A gift for:

T0123873

From:

Helen Exley

If you love this book…

…you will probably want to know how to find other

books like it. They're all listed on

www.helenexley.com

Helen Exley and her team have specialised in creating gifts
between families, friends and loved ones…
A major part of Helen's work has been to bring love and communication
within families by finding and publishing the things people everywhere
would like to say to the people they love.
Her books obviously strike a chord because they are now
distributed in more than eighty countries.

You can follow us on ▪ and ▪

JANUARY 1

In the depth of winter, I finally learned that within me there lay an invincible summer.

ALBERT CAMUS 1913 – 1960

EDITED BY DALTON EXLEY
PHOTOGRAPHY BY RICHARD EXLEY

Published in 2015 and 2021 by Helen Exley® LONDON in Great Britain.
All the words by Pam Brown, Dalton Exley, Charlotte Gray, Peter Gray,
Stuart & Linda MacFarlane are copyright © Helen Exley Creative Ltd 2015, 2021.
Excerpts by Professor Paula Giddings,
EA Woodson Professor of Africana Studies, Smith College.
Photography by Richard Exley © Helen Exley Creative Ltd 2015, 2021.
Design, selection and arrangement © Helen Exley Creative Ltd 2015, 2021.

ISBN 978-1-84634-989-8

12   11   10   9   8   7   6   5   4   3   2   1

Helen Exley® LONDON
16 Chalk Hill, Watford, Hertfordshire, WD19 4BG, UK
www.helenexley.com

Every day you must say to yourself,
"Today I am going to begin."

JEAN PIERRE DE CAUSSADE S.J. 1675 – 1751

For every wound, the ointment of time.

WELSH PROVERB

JANUARY 3

To know and yet think
we do not know
is the highest attainment,
not to know and yet
think we do know
is a disease.

LAO TZU 604 B.C. – 531 B.C.

DECEMBER 30

During my eighty-seven
years I have witnessed
a whole succession
of technological revolutions.
But none of them has done
away with the need for
character in the individual
or the ability to think.

BERNARD M. BARUCH
1870 – 1965

JANUARY 4

Never mistake
knowledge for wisdom.
One helps you
make a living;
the other helps you
make a life.

SANDRA CAREY

Do nondoing, strive for nonstriving, savour the flavourless, regard the small as important, make much of little, repay enmity with virtue; plan for difficulty when it is still easy, do the great while it is still small.

LAO TZU 604 B.C. - 531 B.C.

THOSE IN A HURRY DO NOT ARRIVE.

ZEN WISDOM

DECEMBER 28

Do not weep; do not wax indignant. Understand.

BENEDICT BARUCH SPINOZA
1632 – 1677

JANUARY 6

THE PASSING
MINUTE
IS EVERY
PERSON'S
EQUAL
POSSESSION.

MARCUS AURELIUS
A.D. 121 – 180

DECEMBER 27

JOY AND SORROW ARE LIFE'S COMPANIONS.

JAPANESE PROVERB

JANUARY 7

Plan for the difficult while it is easy;
Act on the large while it's minute.
The most difficult things in the world begin
with things that are easy.

LAO TZU 604 B.C. – 531 B.C.

DECEMBER 26

The most visible creators
I know of are those artists whose
medium is life itself. The ones who
express the inexpressible – without
brush, hammer, clay, or guitar.
Whatever their presence touches
has increased life.

J. STONE

JANUARY 8

How we spend our days is,
of course, how we spend our lives.

ANNIE DILLARD, B. 1945

DECEMBER 25

Reflect upon your blessings,
of which every man has plenty, not on your past misfortunes,
of which all men have some.

CHARLES DICKENS 1812 – 1870

Take a chance! All life is a chance.
The one who goes furthest is generally the one
who is willing to do and dare.

DALE CARNEGIE 1888 – 1955

Peace between us begins with the cessation of againstness.

K. BRADFORD BROWN

As long as you live,
keep learning how to live.

SENECA THE YOUNGER
4 B.C. – A.D. 65

There is a wisdom at the heart of things.
And we, frail, silly frightened creatures that we are,
are part of it. Do not be afraid.

PETER GRAY

JANUARY 11

Wisdom is
to discover
what really matters
and let go the rest.

PAM BROWN 1928 – 2014

DECEMBER 22

Never bear more
than one kind of trouble
at a time.
Some people bear three
– all they have had,
all they have now,
and all they
expect to have.

EDWARD EVERETT HALE
1822 – 1909

JANUARY 12

To understand all
is to forgive all.

MADAME DE STAEL

DECEMBER 21

... Misfortune and destruction
are not final.
When the grass has been burnt
by the fire of the steppe,
it will grow
anew in summer.

MONGOLIAN WISDOM

JANUARY 13

We must decide
on what we will not do,
and then we will be
able to act with vigour
in what we ought to do.

MENCIUS 371 B.C. – 289 B.C.

DECEMBER 20

I am enough of an artist
to draw freely upon
my imagination.
Imagination is more
important than knowledge.
Knowledge is limited.
Imagination encircles
the world.

ALBERT EINSTEIN
1879 – 1955

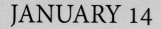

A good head and a good heart
are always a formidable combination.

NELSON ROLIHLAHLA MANDELA
1918 – 2013

The glory is not in never falling,
but in rising every time you fall.

CHINESE PROVERB

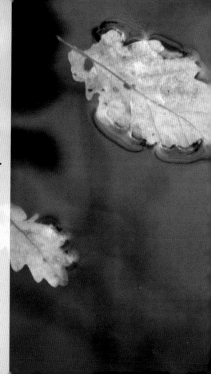

JANUARY 15

None of us can ever
go back in time
and start anything again.
What we can all do,
if we want to,
is start again from now
and make
a brand new ending.

DR. DALTON EXLEY

DECEMBER 18

Happiness is the
art of making a
bouquet of those
flowers within reach.
BOB GODDARD

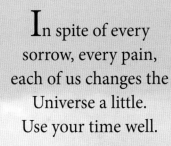

JANUARY 16

In spite of every sorrow, every pain, each of us changes the Universe a little. Use your time well.

PAM BROWN 1928 – 2014

DECEMBER 17

Millions long
for immortality
who do not know
what to do
with themselves
on a rainy
Sunday afternoon.

SUSAN ERTZ 1894 – 1985

JANUARY 17

The fairest thing
we can experience
is the mysterious.
It is the fundamental
emotion which stands
at the cradle
of true art and
true science.

ALBERT EINSTEIN
1879 – 1955

DECEMBER 16

ANYONE
WHO KEEPS THE ABILITY
TO SEE BEAUTY
NEVER GROWS OLD.

FRANZ KAFKA 1883 – 1924

At the end of a difficult day,
congratulate yourself on your achievements
no matter how small they may seem.
Celebrate your life.
Tomorrow is another day in that life and you
deserve it to be a happy and successful day.

STUART & LINDA MACFARLANE

DECEMBER 15

In the end possessions
mean nothing, ambition
is a childish fantasy.
Even beauty blurs –
so that all things
come together
in a new perception.
And only love is left.

CHARLOTTE GRAY

JANUARY 19

Wisdom means keeping
a sense of the fallibility
of all our views
and opinions,
and the uncertainty
and instability of
the things we count on.

GERALD BRENAN
1894 – 1987

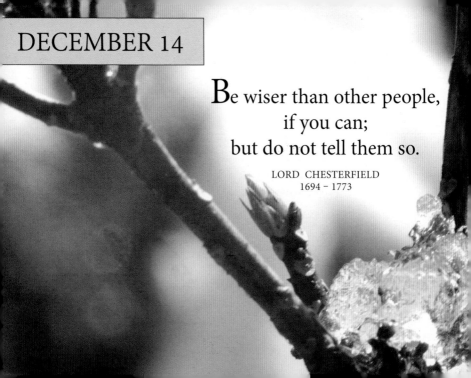

DECEMBER 14

Be wiser than other people,
if you can;
but do not tell them so.

LORD CHESTERFIELD
1694 – 1773

JANUARY 20

Time is really the only capital that any human being has
and the only thing we can't afford to lose.

THOMAS EDISON 1847 – 1931

DECEMBER 13

In the end, just three things matter:
How well we have lived
How well we have loved
How well we have learned to let go.

JACK KORNFIELD

JANUARY 21

If you were going to die soon and had only one phone call you could make, who would you call and what would you say? And why are you waiting?

STEPHEN LEVINE, B. 1937

DECEMBER 12

Finish every day and be done with it...
You have done what you could; some blunders and absurdities
no doubt crept in; forget them as soon as you can...
This day is all that is good and fair. It is too dear,
with its hopes and invitations, to waste a moment on yesterdays.

RALPH WALDO EMERSON 1803 – 1882

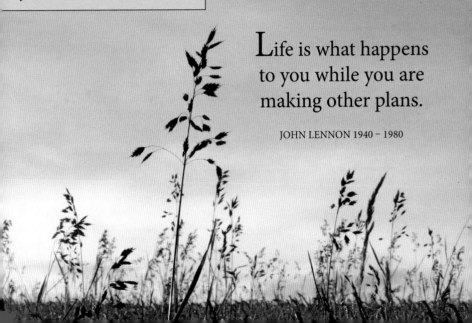

JANUARY 22

Life is what happens to you while you are making other plans.

JOHN LENNON 1940 – 1980

DECEMBER 11

If we examine our thoughts,
we shall find them to be set on the past
and the future. Of the present
we think hardly at all, and if we do,
it is only that we may draw from it
a light wherewith to control
the future. Thus we never live,
but we hope to live; and it is
inevitable that, ever preparing
to be happy, we never are so.

BLAISE PASCAL 1623 – 1662

JANUARY 23

We shall be made
truly wise if we
be made content;
content, too,
not only with what
we can understand,
but content with
what we do not
understand...

CHARLES KINGSLEY
1819 – 1875

It has never been, and never will be easy work!
But the road that is built in hope is more pleasant
to the traveler than the road built in despair,
even though they both lead to the same destination

MARION ZIMMER BRADLEY 1930 – 1999

It's only when we truly know
and understand that we have
a limited time on earth –
and that we have no way of knowing
when our time is up – that we will
begin to live each day to the fullest,
as if it was the only one we had.

ELISABETH KÜBLER-ROSS
1926 – 2004

DECEMBER 9

You can make more friends
in two months
by becoming interested
in other people
than you can in two years
by trying to get people
interested in you.

DALE CARNEGIE
1888 – 1955

If you don't like something about yourself, change it. If you can't change it, accept it.

TED SHACKELFORD

The greatest truths are the simplest,
and so are the greatest people.

J. C. HARE

Wisdom is the finest beauty of a person.

NIGERIAN YORUBA ORACLE

Everything flows, and nothing stays still.

HERACLITUS 535 B.C. - 475 B.C.

A new life begins for us with every second.
Let us go forward joyously to meet it.
We must press on, whether we will or no,
and we shall walk better with our eyes before us
than with them ever cast behind.

JEROME K. JEROME 1859 – 1927

DECEMBER 6

Hold on; hold fast;
hold out.
Patience is genius.

COMTE DE BUFFON 1707 – 1788

JANUARY 28

It is indeed foolish
to be unhappy
now because you may
be unhappy
at some future time.

SENECA THE YOUNGER
4 B.C. – A.D. 65

What does not kill you
makes you stronger.

PROVERB

JANUARY 29

We make a living
by what we get,
but we make a life
by what we give.

SIR WINSTON CHURCHILL
1874 – 1965

DECEMBER 4

OUR REMEDIES
OFT IN
OURSELVES DO LIE.

WILLIAM SHAKESPEARE
1564 – 1616

JANUARY 30

The surest happiness is found
in doing the best you can with what you have.

PAM BROWN 1928 – 2014

DECEMBER 3

The harmony and friendship that we need in our families, nations, and the world can be achieved only through compassion and kindness.

THE DALAI LAMA, B. 1935

In a hundred
mile march,
ninety is about
the halfway
point.

CHINESE PROVERB

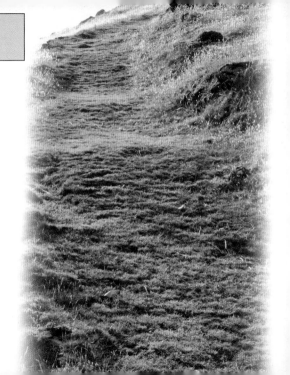

Some people are making
such thorough plans
for rainy days that they aren't
enjoying today's sunshine.

WILLIAM FEATHER 1908 –1976

FEBRUARY 1

It is easy in the world to live after the world's opinion;
it is easy in solitude to live after our own;
but the great person is the one who in the midst
of the crowd keeps with perfect sweetness
the independence of solitude.

RALPH WALDO EMERSON 1803 – 1882

DECEMBER 1

Happiness comes from entering into whatever
we have to do, whether it's watching kids, cleaning the stove,
mowing the lawn. Being happy means entering
wholeheartedly into everything –
no matter what type of challenge it presents,
no matter what the possible difficulties involved –
entering into it body and soul, mind and spirit.

MONKS OF SKETE

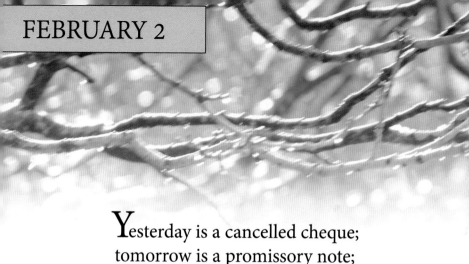

FEBRUARY 2

Yesterday is a cancelled cheque;
tomorrow is a promissory note;
today is the only cash you have –
so spend it wisely.

KAY LYONS

Do not suppose opportunity will knock twice at your door.

SEBASTIEN CHAMFORT 1741 – 1794

FEBRUARY 3

What to do
with a mistake –
recognize it,
admit it,
learn from it,
forget it.

DEAN SMITH

NOVEMBER 29

The wise man travels
to discover himself.

JAMES RUSSELL LOWELL 1819 – 1891

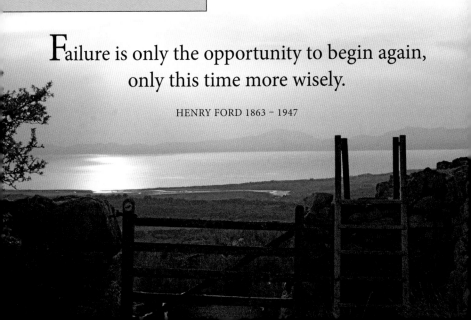

FEBRUARY 4

Failure is only the opportunity to begin again,
only this time more wisely.

HENRY FORD 1863 – 1947

The crowning fortune
is to be born to some pursuit
which finds you employment
and happiness,
whether it be to make
baskets or broadswords,
or canals, or statues,
or songs.

RALPH WALDO EMERSON
1803 – 1882

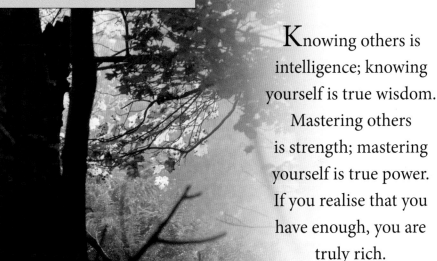

FEBRUARY 5

Knowing others is
intelligence; knowing
yourself is true wisdom.
Mastering others
is strength; mastering
yourself is true power.
If you realise that you
have enough, you are
truly rich.

"TAO TE CHING"

That is happiness: to be dissolved
into something complete and great.

WILLA CATHER 1873 – 1947

FEBRUARY 6

Wisdom is often-times nearer when we stoop
than when we soar.

WILLIAM WORDSWORTH
1770 – 1850

THE ART OF BEING WISE
IS KNOWING WHAT TO OVERLOOK.

WILLIAM JAMES 1842–1910

FEBRUARY 7

Nobody
ever died of
laughter.

MAX BEERBOHM
1872 – 1956

Life is a great
bundle of
little things.

OLIVER WENDELL HOLMES JR.
1841 – 1935

Live your Joy, go against the grain.
Don't be made timid by worried rejection.
Let nature's curious wisdom fill you.
Let the world's mystical heritage guide you.
Paint your canvases, play your tunes.

SIR THOMAS MORE 1478 – 1535

NOVEMBER 24

Do not rush toward
your dream at such
a speed that your feet
ache and the scenery
is reduced to a blur.
Slow down, enjoy the
journey and the dream
will come to you.

STUART & LINDA
MACFARLANE

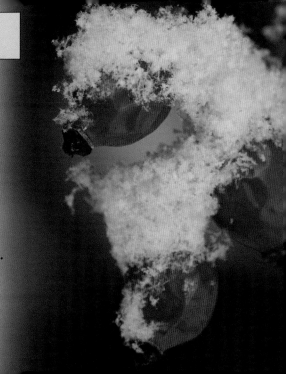

FEBRUARY 9

In quietness
one comes to know
that nothing good
is ever lost.
It has become a part
of all that is,
and all that is to come.

PAM BROWN 1928 - 2014

Don't ask yourself what the world needs.
Ask yourself what makes you come alive,
and go do that, because what the world needs
is people who have come alive.

HOWARD THURMAN

FEBRUARY 10

The invariable mark
of wisdom
is to see the miraculous
in the common.

RALPH WALDO EMERSON
1803 – 1882

It is the wisest who grieve most at the loss of time.

DANTE

FEBRUARY 11

Einstein's three rules of work:

1) Out of clutter find simplicity.
2) From discord make harmony.
3) In the middle of difficulty lies opportunity.

ALBERT EINSTEIN 1879 – 1955

To fill the hour – that is happiness;
to fill the hour, and leave no crevice for a repentance
or an approval.

RALPH WALDO EMERSON 1803 – 1882

FEBRUARY 12

The more
you learn,
the sooner
you will know
how little
you know.

ISABEL ALLENDE,
B. 1942

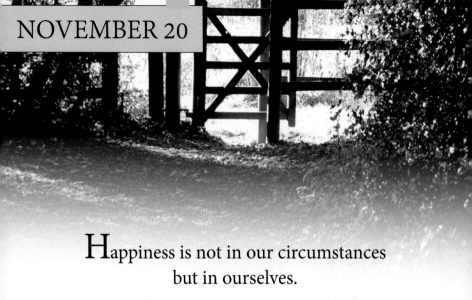

Happiness is not in our circumstances
but in ourselves.

FROM "THE FRIENDSHIP BOOK OF FRANCIS GAY"

FEBRUARY 13

We're perhaps not really
so sophisticated and so very different
from people down the ages
as we like to think we are.
Much the same fears, desires,
loves and hopes link humankind
down through the centuries.
It reminds us to sometimes pause
a little and see what's
really important in our lives.

DR. DALTON EXLEY

NOVEMBER 19

Real love begins
where nothing is expected
in return.

ANTOINE DE SAINT-EXUPERY
1900 – 1944

FEBRUARY 14

MAKE YOURSELF
NECESSARY
TO SOMEBODY.

RALPH WALDO EMERSON
1803 – 1882

Be more concerned with your character than your reputation, because your character is what you really are, while your reputation is merely what others think you are.

JOHN WOODEN
1910 – 2010

FEBRUARY 15

Real knowledge is to know
the extent of one's ignorance.

CONFUCIUS 551 B.C. – 479 B.C.

NOVEMBER 17

When the great joys
evade you
cherish the little ones.

PAM BROWN 1928 - 2014

FEBRUARY 16

Live in the present,
do all the things that
need to be done.
Do all the good
you can each day.
The future will unfold.

PEACE PILGRIM

NOVEMBER 16

It's better to light a candle than to curse the darkness.

ELEANOR ROOSEVELT 1884 – 1962

FEBRUARY 17

...those who know the value
and the exquisite taste
of solitary freedom
(for one is only free
when one is alone)...

ISABELLE EBERHARDT
1877 – 1904

It is not what happens to you
in life that counts but how
you play the cards you are dealt.

HELEN FIELDING, B. 1958

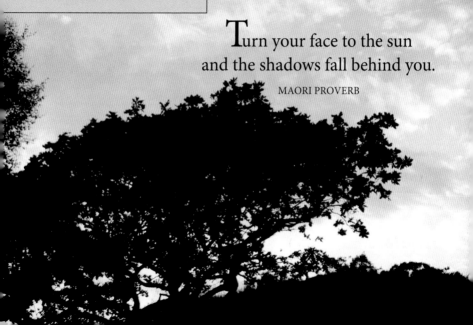

FEBRUARY 18

Turn your face to the sun
and the shadows fall behind you.

MAORI PROVERB

NOVEMBER 14

Every now and again
examine what you have
accepted as the truth.
You may be astounded.

PAM BROWN 1928 – 2014

FEBRUARY 19

If you concentrate on finding whatever is good in every situation, you will discover that your life will suddenly be filled with gratitude, a feeling that nurtures the soul.

RABBI HAROLD KUSHNER

NOVEMBER 13

"This too will pass." I was taught
these words by my grandmother as
a phrase that is to be used at all times
in your life. When things are
spectacularly dreadful; when things
are absolutely appalling;
when everything is superb and
wonderful and marvellous and happy
– say these four words to yourself.
They will give you a sense of
perspective and help you also to make
the most of what is good and be stoical
about what is bad.

CLAIRE RAYNER 1931 – 2010

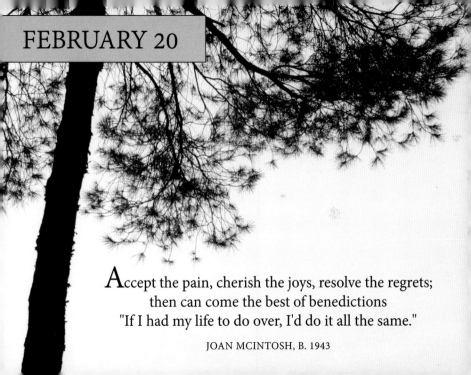

FEBRUARY 20

Accept the pain, cherish the joys, resolve the regrets;
then can come the best of benedictions
"If I had my life to do over, I'd do it all the same."

JOAN MCINTOSH, B. 1943

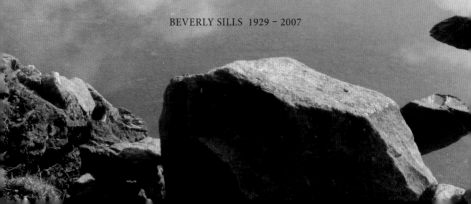

NOVEMBER 12

It seemed no longer important whether everyone
loved me or not – more important now was for me to love them.
Feeling that way turns your whole life around,
living becomes the act of giving.

BEVERLY SILLS 1929 – 2007

FEBRUARY 21

Happiness
is self-derived and
self-created.

ELLEN GILCHRIST

NOVEMBER 11

WE ARE ALWAYS
GETTING READY
TO LIVE,
BUT NEVER LIVING.

RALPH WALDO EMERSON
1803 – 1882

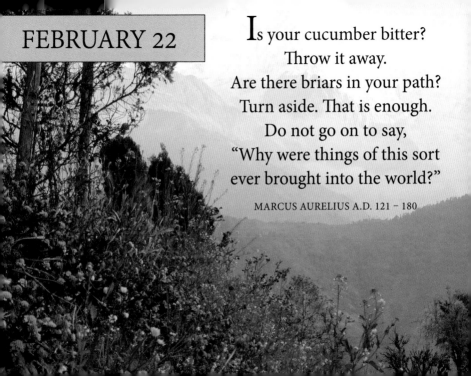

FEBRUARY 22

Is your cucumber bitter?
Throw it away.
Are there briars in your path?
Turn aside. That is enough.
Do not go on to say,
"Why were things of this sort
ever brought into the world?"

MARCUS AURELIUS A.D. 121 – 180

Things I longed for in vain and things
that I got – let them pass.
Let me but truly possess the things that I ever
spurned and overlooked.

RABINDRANATH TAGORE
1861 – 1941

I want to beg you, as much as I can, to be patient toward all that is unsolved in your heart and to try to love the questions themselves like locked rooms and like books that are written in a very foreign tongue. Do not seek the answers, which cannot be given you, because you would not be able to live them. And the point is to live everything.
Live the questions now.

RAINER MARIA RILKE 1875 – 1926

NOVEMBER 9

W e need time to dream,
time to remember, and time to reach the infinite.
Time to be.

GLADYS TABER 1899 – 1980

FEBRUARY 24

WHEN YOU
HAVE FAULTS,
DO NOT FEAR TO
ABANDON THEM.

CONFUCIUS
551 B.C – 479 B.C.

WE CAN BE
VALUED ONLY AS
WE MAKE OURSELVES
VALUABLE.

RALPH WALDO EMERSON
1803 – 1882

It is tranquil people who accomplish much.

HENRY DAVID THOREAU 1817 – 1862

NOVEMBER 7

Contentment is the philosopher's stone,
which turns all it toucheth into gold;
the poor man is rich with it, the rich man
poor without it.

PROVERB

I bequeath myself to the dirt
to grow from the grass I love,
If you want me again
look for me under your boot-soles.

WALT WHITMAN 1819 – 1892

NOVEMBER 6

Always we hope
someone else has the answer.
Some other place will be better,
some other time
it will all turn out well.

This is it.
No one else has the answer.
No other place will be better,
and it has already turned out.

At the centre of your being
you have the answer;
you know who you are
and you know what you want.

LAO TZU 604 B.C. – 531 B.C.

FEBRUARY 27

We are such a very little
raft adrift among the stars.
How foolish for us to argue
among ourselves.
We can quarrel
and be lost, or work
together and survive.

PAM BROWN 1928 – 2014

NOVEMBER 5

Then and there I invented
this rule for myself to be applied
to every decision I might have
to make in the future. I would sort
out all the arguments and see which
belonged to fear and which
to creativeness, and other things
being equal I would make
the decision which had
the larger number of
creative reasons on its side.

KATHARINE BUTLER HATHAWAY
1890 – 1942

Keep in mind
that neither success nor
failure is ever final.

ROGER BABSON

The only difference between a rut
and a grave is their dimensions.

ELLEN GLASGOW 1874 - 1945

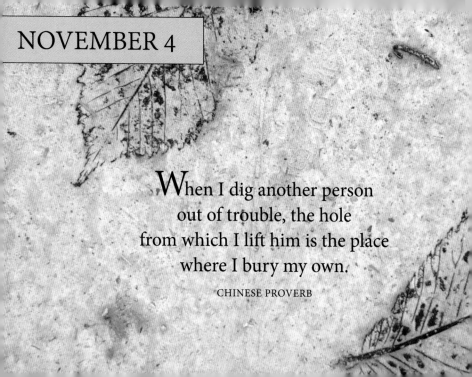

When I dig another person
out of trouble, the hole
from which I lift him is the place
where I bury my own.

CHINESE PROVERB

The trees that are slow to grow bear the best fruit.

MOLIÈRE 1622 – 1673

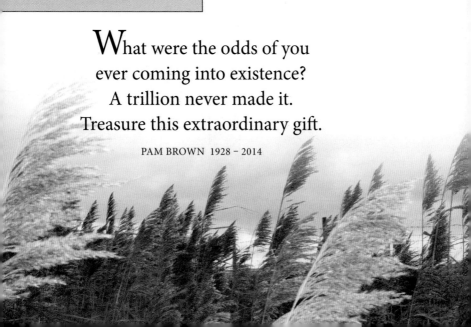

NOVEMBER 3

What were the odds of you
ever coming into existence?
A trillion never made it.
Treasure this extraordinary gift.

PAM BROWN 1928 – 2014

MARCH 2

Take time to be friendly – It is the road to happiness.

Take time to dream – It is hitching your wagon to a star.

Take time to love and to be loved – It is the privilege of the gods.

Take time to look around – It is too short a day to be selfish.

Take time to laugh – It is the music of the soul.

FROM AN OLD ENGLISH SAMPLER

NOVEMBER 2

Manifest
plainness,
Embrace
simplicity,
Reduce
selfishness,
Have few
desires.

LAO TZU
604 B.C. – 531 B.C.

You have to have hope
in your heart, but you have
to nurture it too.
It's like love, you can't just
take it all for granted.
No, you have to work at it.

DR. DALTON EXLEY

NOVEMBER 1

Knowledge was inherent
in all things. The world
was a library and its books
were the stones, leaves,
grass, brooks...
We learned to do what
only the students of nature
ever learn, and that was
to feel beauty.

LUTHER STANDING BEAR
(OGLALA SIOUX CHIEF)
1868 – 1939

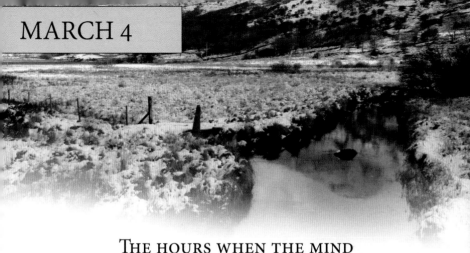

THE HOURS WHEN THE MIND
IS ABSORBED BY BEAUTY
ARE THE ONLY HOURS WE LIVE.

RICHARD JEFFERIES 1848 – 1887

OCTOBER 31

To compose our
character is our
duty...
Our great and
glorious
masterpiece is to
live appropriately.
All other things,
to rule,
to lay up treasure,
to build,
are at most but
little appendices
and props...

MICHEL DE MONTAIGNE
1533–1592

MARCH 5

Don't worry about failure. Worry about the chances you miss when you don't even try.

AUTHOR UNKNOWN

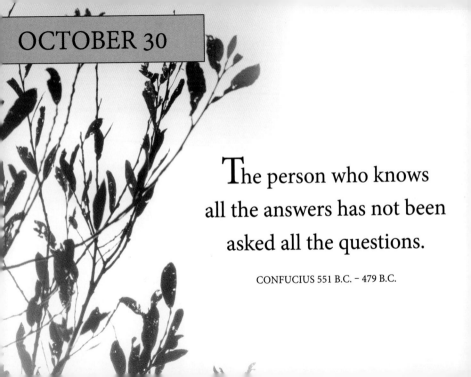

The person who knows
all the answers has not been
asked all the questions.

CONFUCIUS 551 B.C. – 479 B.C.

MARCH 6

IF WE WAIT TILL WE'RE READY,
WE NEVER DO ANYTHING.

ELEANOR ROOSEVELT
1884 – 1962

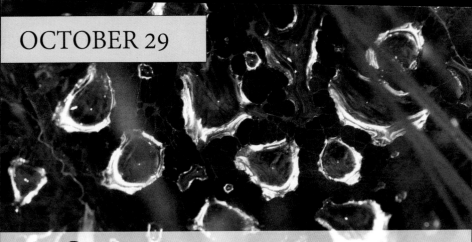

OCTOBER 29

Such words as "death" and "suffering" and "eternity" are best forgotten. We have to become as simple and as wordless as the growing corn or the falling rain. We must just be.

ETTY HILLESUM 1914 – 1943

MARCH 7

Life is the first gift,
love is the second,
and understanding
the third.

MARGE PIERCY, B. 1936

OCTOBER 28

The strong, calm person
is always loved and
revered. He is like
a shade-giving tree
in a thirsty land,
or a sheltering rock
in a storm.

JAMES ALLEN 1864 – 1912

MARCH 8

Your wealth can be stolen,
but the precious riches buried deep
in your soul cannot.

MINNIE RIPERTON 1947 – 1979

OCTOBER 27

BY SWALLOWING
EVIL WORDS UNSAID,
NO ONE HAS EVER
HARMED
HIS STOMACH.

SIR WINSTON CHURCHILL
1874 – 1965

MARCH 9

TO FIND WISDOM
ONE MUST FIRST
DISCOVER SILENCE.

PAM BROWN 1928 – 2014

Failure may not mean
absolute failure.
The failed artist has gained
perception, new depths of
understanding, greater skills.
The failed musician hears
another's work with sharper
perception than any layman could.
To learn is to live.
Nothing is wasted.

PAM BROWN 1928 – 2014

MARCH 10

*It is good to be alone
in a garden at dawn
or dark so that all its
shy presences may
haunt you
and possess you
in a reverie of
suspended thought.*

JAMES DOUGLAS

OCTOBER 25

Truth does not happen, it just is.

HOPI

Optimism is the faith that leads
to achievement. Nothing can be done
without hope and confidence.

HELEN KELLER 1880 – 1968

Complete possession is proved
only by giving.
All you are unable to give possesses you.

ANDRÉ GIDE 1861 – 1951

MARCH 12

To receive everything, one must open one's hands and give.

TAISEN DESHIMARU

OCTOBER 23

THE LACK OF
KNOWLEDGE
IS DARKER
THAN NIGHT.

AFRICAN PROVERB

MARCH 13

Even if I knew certainly
the world would end tomorrow,
I would plant an apple tree today.

MARTIN LUTHER 1483 – 1546

To live as fully, as completely
as possible, to be happy...
is the true aim and end to life.

LLEWELYN POWYS

Marvels lie under
your hand.
Only look and you
will find them.

PAM BROWN 1928 – 2014

OCTOBER 21

REMEMBER
THAT YOUR
WORDS CAN
DEEPLY HURT.
REMEMBER
THAT YOUR
WORDS CAN
QUICKLY HEAL.

H. JACKSON BROWN JR.

MARCH 15

You've got to find what you love and that is as true for work as it is for lovers... If you haven't found it yet, keep looking and don't settle. As with all matters of the heart, you'll know when you've found it.

STEVE JOBS 1955 – 2011

OCTOBER 20

Expect trouble as
an inevitable part of life
and when it comes,
hold your head high,
look it squarely in the eye
and say "I will be bigger than
you. You cannot defeat me."
Then repeat to yourself
the most comforting words,
"This too shall pass."

ANN LANDERS

Failure brings experience and experience wisdom.

AUTHOR UNKNOWN

You shall be free indeed when your days are not without
a care nor your nights without a want and a grief,
But rather when these things girdle your life and yet you rise
above them naked and unbound.

KAHLIL GIBRAN 1883 – 1931

The ideals, which have lighted my way, and time after time have given me new courage to face life cheerfully, have been kindness, beauty, and truth… The trite subjects of human efforts – possessions, outward success, luxury – have always seemed to me contemptible.

ALBERT EINSTEIN 1879 – 1955

OCTOBER 18

The man who preserves
his selfhood ever calm and unshaken
by the storms of existence...
If you ask: "What are the fruits
of silence?" he will say:
"They are self-control, true courage
or endurance, patience, dignity,
and reverence. Silence is
the corner-stone of character."

OHIYESA
(DR. CHARLES ALEXANDER EASTMAN)
1858 – 1939

To live a good and simple life
one must take the variety
and subtlety and astonishment
of existence and translate it
into clear, glad acceptance.

PAM BROWN 1928 –2014

When you assume
there is no hope,
you guarantee
there will
be no hope.

NOAM CHOMSKY,
B. 1928

To know what
you know
and know what you
don't know
is characteristic
of one who knows.

CONFUCIUS 551 B.C. – 479 B.C.

Always be kind, for everyone is fighting a hard battle.

PLATO c.427 B.C. – 347 B.C.

There is nothing ordinary.
There is a wonder
and a complexity
in the smallest thing.

PAM BROWN 1928 – 2014

OCTOBER 15

Twenty years from now you will be more disappointed by things that you didn't do than the ones you did do. So throw off the bowlines. Sail away from safe harbor. Catch the trade winds in your sails. Explore. Dream. Discover.

MARK TWAIN 1835 –1910

MARCH 21

Do a little more than you
have to, more than
your share, and do it
as well as you can.

RALPH CHARELL

OCTOBER 14

They are wise
who do not grieve
for the things
which they don't have,
but rejoice
for those which
they have.

EPICTETUS c.55 – 135

Don't judge each day by the harvest you reap,
but by the seeds that you plant.

ROBERT LOUIS STEVENSON 1850 – 1894

OCTOBER 13

Let us spend one day
as deliberately as nature,
and not be thrown off
the track by every nutshell
and mosquito's wing that falls
on the rails. Let us rise early
and fast, or break fast, gently
and without perturbation.
If the engine whistles,
let it whistle till it is hoarse
for its pains. If the bell rings,
why should we run?

HENRY DAVID THOREAU
1817 – 1862

MARCH 23

To change one's mind
can be a painful business.
But if long consideration
and total honesty lead you
from a relationship, a faith
or a career – you must go.
To live a lie diminishes
everyone involved.

PAM BROWN 1928 – 2014

OCTOBER 12

Less is more.

ROBERT BROWNING 1812 - 1889

MARCH 24

TO THE MIND
THAT IS STILL,
THE WHOLE UNIVERSE
SURRENDERS.

CHUANG TZU 369 B.C. – 286 B.C.

OCTOBER 11

It had been my repeated
experience that when you
said to life calmly and
firmly (but very firmly!),
"I trust you; do what you
must," life had an uncanny
way of responding
to your need.

OLGA ILYIN

Even the saddest things
can become, once we have
made peace with them,
a source of wisdom
and strength for the journey
that still lies ahead.

FREDERICK BUECHNER,
B. 1926

Your pain is the breaking of the shell that encloses your
understanding. Even as the stone of the fruit must break,
that its heart may stand in the sun, so you must know pain.
And could you keep your heart in wonder at the daily miracles
of your life, your pain would not seem less wondrous than your joy;
And you would accept the seasons of your heart.

KAHLIL GIBRAN 1883–1931

MARCH 26

If there be righteousness
in the heart,
there will be beauty
in the character.
If there be beauty
in the character,
there will be harmony
in the home.
If there be harmony
in the home,
there will be order
in the nation.
If there be order
in the nation,
there will be peace
in the world.

CONFUCIUS 551 B.C. – 479 B.C.

THERE IS NO
GREATER GIFT
THAN THAT OF
SHARING
WISDOM AND LOVE.

MARYBETH BOND

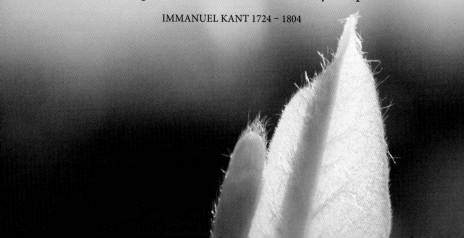

MARCH 27

All the interests of our reason, speculative as well as practical,
combine in the following three questions: What can I know?
What ought I to do? And for what may I hope?

IMMANUEL KANT 1724 – 1804

I have never met a man
so ignorant that I couldn't learn
something from him.

GALILEO 1564 – 1642

HAPPINESS

DEPENDS

UPON

OURSELVES.

ARISTOTLE 384 B.C. – 322 B.C.

OCTOBER 7

THE TRUE PRIZE
IS WISDOM –
THE TRUE TREASURE
IS PEACE.

STUART & LINDA MACFARLANE

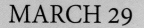

Though nothing can bring back
the hour of splendour in the grass,
of glory in the flower;
we will grieve not, rather find
strength in what remains behind.

WILLIAM WORDSWORTH
1770 – 1850

OCTOBER 6

Successful living is a triumph over confusion.

AUTHOR UNKNOWN

MARCH 30

Contentment…

Comes as the infallible result of great acceptances, great humilities
– of not trying to make ourselves this or that (to conform to some
dramatized version of ourselves), but of surrendering ourselves to
the fullness of life – of letting life flow through us.

DAVID GRAYSON

OCTOBER 5

...if you want something very badly, you can achieve it.
It may take patience, very hard work,
a real struggle, and a long time - but it can be done.
That much faith is a prerequisite of any undertaking,
artistic or otherwise.

He who stops completely
before taking the next step will spend a lifetime
standing on one leg.

CHINESE PROVERB

OCTOBER 4

Things never go
so well that one
should have no fear,
and never so
ill that one
should have no hope.

TURKISH PROVERB

Listen! Or your tongue will make you deaf.

CHEROKEE SAYING

OCTOBER 3

We see it like this: it is as if we are all in a canoe travelling through time. If someone begins to make a fire in their part of the canoe, and another begins to pour water inside the canoe, it will affect us all. And it is the responsibility of each person in the canoe to ensure that it is not destroyed. Our planet is like one big canoe travelling through time.

AILTON KRENAK
Campaigner for the indigenous people of the Amazon

APRIL 2

How many cares one loses when one decides not to be something, but to be someone.

COCO CHANEL 1883 – 1971

OCTOBER 2

Learn by practice.
Whether it means
to learn to dance
by practicing dancing
or to live by
practicing living,
the principles
are the same.

MARTHA GRAHAM
1894 – 1991

The door of happiness
does not open away from us:
we cannot rush at it
to push it open.
It opens towards us and,
therefore, nothing is
required of us.

SØREN KIERKEGAARD
1813 – 1855

Be not too critical of others, and love much.

JULIAN HUXLEY

Let us follow our destiny,
ebb and flow.
Whatever may happen,
we master fortune
by accepting it.

VIRGIL 70 B.C. – 19 B.C.

SEPTEMBER 30

ONE MUST NEVER BE IN HASTE TO END A DAY;
THERE ARE TOO FEW OF THEM IN A LIFETIME.

DALE CONMAN

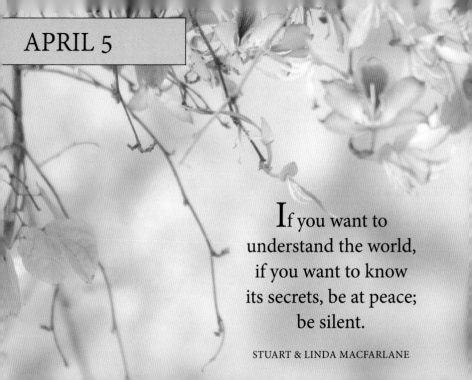

APRIL 5

If you want to
understand the world,
if you want to know
its secrets, be at peace;
be silent.

STUART & LINDA MACFARLANE

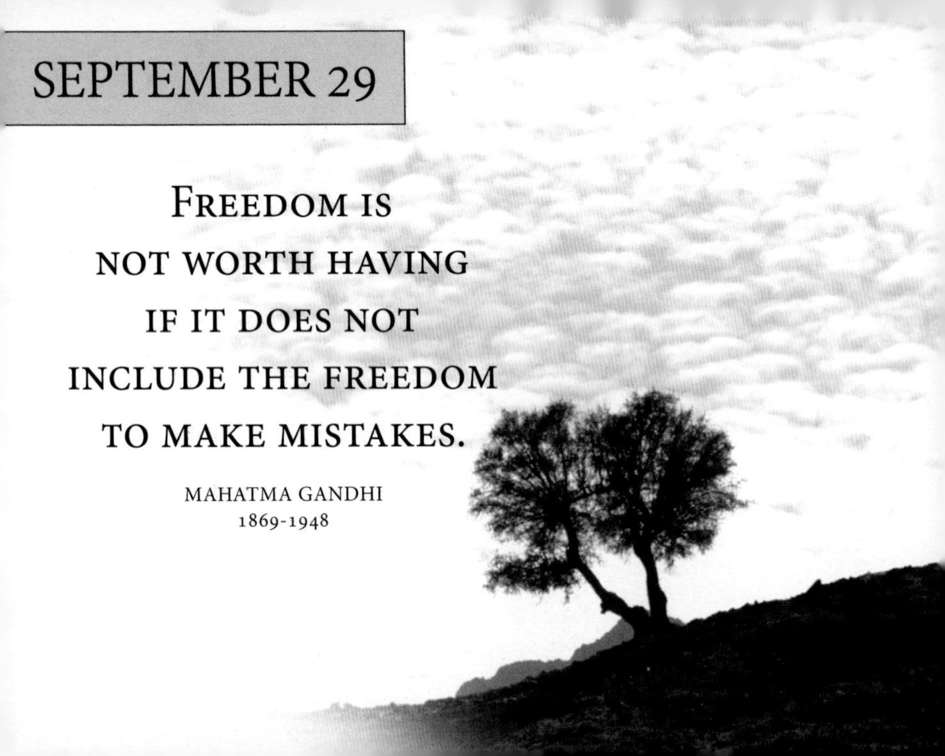

SEPTEMBER 29

FREEDOM IS
NOT WORTH HAVING
IF IT DOES NOT
INCLUDE THE FREEDOM
TO MAKE MISTAKES.

MAHATMA GANDHI
1869-1948

APRIL 6

The only gift is a portion of yourself.

RALPH WALDO EMERSON 1803 – 1882

SEPTEMBER 28

Most people seek after
what they do not possess
and are then enslaved
by the very things they
want to acquire.
Only when one has ceased
to need things can you
truly be your own master
and really exist.

ANWAR SADAT 1918 – 1981

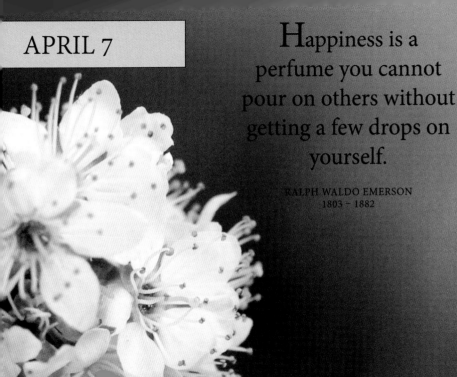

APRIL 7

Happiness is a
perfume you cannot
pour on others without
getting a few drops on
yourself.

RALPH WALDO EMERSON
1803 – 1882

Sorrow, disappointment, failure
– learn from them and let them go.

PAM BROWN 1928 – 2014

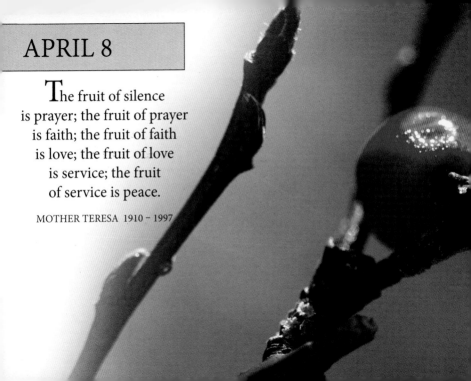

APRIL 8

The fruit of silence
is prayer; the fruit of prayer
is faith; the fruit of faith
is love; the fruit of love
is service; the fruit
of service is peace.

MOTHER TERESA 1910 – 1997

SEPTEMBER 26

Tomorrow's
life is too late.
Live today.

MARTIAL C.40 – C.104

APRIL 9

To everything there is a season, and a time to every purpose
under heaven: a time to be born, and a time to die;
a time to plant, and a time to pluck up that which is planted;
a time to kill, and a time to heal; a time to break down,
and a time to build up; a time to weep, and a time to laugh;
a time to mourn, and a time to dance...

ECCLESIASTES 3:1–8

The wise
do not lay up
their own treasures.
The more they give
to others,
the more they have.

LAO TZU 604 B.C.– 531B.C.

APRIL 10

Life appears to me too short to be spent in nursing animosity or registering wrongs.

CHARLOTTE BRONTË 1816 – 1855

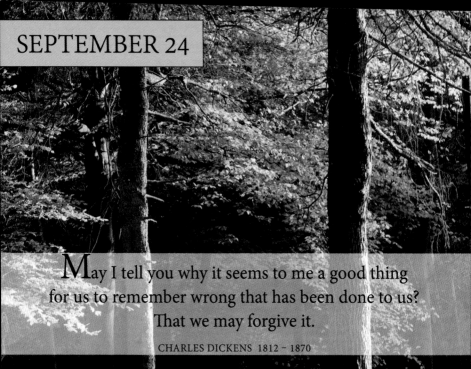

SEPTEMBER 24

May I tell you why it seems to me a good thing
for us to remember wrong that has been done to us?
That we may forgive it.

CHARLES DICKENS 1812 – 1870

Rejoice at your life, for the time is
more advanced than you think.

LAO TZU 604 B.C. – 531 B.C.

SEPTEMBER 23

Life is really simple, but we insist on making it complicated.

CONFUCIUS 551 B.C. - 479 B.C.

APRIL 12

Keep a good heart.
That's the most
important thing
in life.
It's not how much
money you make
or what you
can acquire.
The art of it is
to keep a
good heart.

JONI MITCHELL

SEPTEMBER 22

GRIEF CAN TAKE CARE
OF ITSELF; BUT TO GET
THE FULL VALUE OF JOY,
YOU MUST HAVE
SOMEBODY TO DIVIDE
IT WITH.

MARK TWAIN
1835 – 1910

APRIL 13

Keep your heart free from hate, your mind from worry. Live simply, expect little, give much. Fill your life with love. Scatter sunshine. Forget self, think of others. Do as you would be done by.

NORMAN VINCENT PEALE
1898 – 1993

SEPTEMBER 21

Slow down and enjoy life.
It's not only the scenery
you miss by going too fast
– you also miss the sense of
where you're going and why.

EDDIE CANTOR 1892 – 1964

APRIL 14

It is so hard for us little human beings to accept this deal that we get. We get to live, then we have to die. What we put into every moment is all we have...

GILDA RADNER 1946 – 1989

Work is not always required of us.
There is such a thing as sacred idleness,
the cultivation of which is now fearfully neglected.

GEORGE MACDONALD 1824 – 1905

APRIL 15

Talent is God-given.
Be humble.
Fame is man-given.
Be grateful.
Conceit is self-given.
Be careful.

JOHN WOODEN
1910 – 2010

Come away from the din.
Come away to the quiet fields, over which the great sky
stretches, and where, between us, and the stars,
there lies but silence; and there, in the stillness let us listen
to the voice that is speaking within us.

JEROME K. JEROME 1859 – 1927

APRIL 16

Procrastination
isn't the thief
of time,
but the death
of talent.

PAM BROWN 1928 – 2014

SEPTEMBER 18

There are two tragedies in life. One is not to get your heart's desire. The other is to get it.

GEORGE BERNARD SHAW 1856 - 1950

APRIL 17

Obanije mba ara re je.
One who damages
the character of another
damages his own.

NIGERIAN YORUBA PROVERB

SEPTEMBER 17

We each hold within us a scrap of stardust, a little glory that cannot be destroyed. Whatever dark engulfs us, nothing can put out its light.

PAM BROWN
1928 – 2014

APRIL 18

The acknowledgement
of impermanence holds
within it the key to life itself.

STEPHEN LEVINE, B. 1937

SEPTEMBER 16

I was always
looking outside myself
for strength and
confidence, but it comes
from within.
It is there all the time.

ANNA FREUD 1895 – 1982

APRIL 19

Always direct your thoughts
to those truths
that will give you confidence,
hope, joy, love,
thanksgiving, and turn away
your mind from those
that inspire you with fear,
sadness, depression.

BERTRAND WILBERTFORCE

SEPTEMBER 15

If you concentrate on
finding whatever is good
in every situation,
you will discover that
your life will suddenly
be filled with gratitude,
a feeling that nurtures
the soul.

RABBI HAROLD KUSHNER

APRIL 20

Eating
a little
and
speaking
little
can hurt
no one.

HOPI

Leave home
in the sunshine:
Dance through a meadow
Or sit by a stream
and just be.
The lilt of the water
Will gather your worries
And carry them down
to the sea.

J. DONALD WALTERS 1926 – 2013

APRIL 21

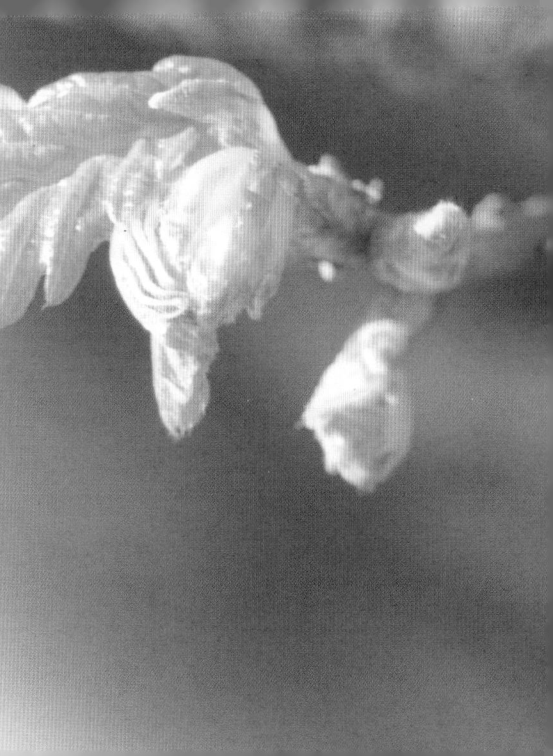

A man lives again through his children, the trees that he has planted, the words that he has uttered.

TRADITIONAL
MASSONGO WORDS

SEPTEMBER 13

ENJOY PRESENT
PLEASURES
IN SUCH A WAY
AS NOT
TO INJURE
FUTURE ONES.

SENECA THE YOUNGER
4 B.C. – A.D. 65

APRIL 22

Do not disregard evil, saying,
"It will not come unto me."
By the falling of drops,
even a water jar is filled;
likewise the fool,
gathering little by little,
fills himself with evil.
Do not disregard merit, saying,
"It will not come unto me."
By the falling of drops,
even a water jar is filled;
likewise the wise man,
gathering little by little,
fills himself with good.

FROM "THE DHAMMAPADA"

SEPTEMBER 12

He who binds to himself a joy
Does the winged life destroy;
But he who kisses the joy as it flies
Lives in eternity's sun rise.

WILLIAM BLAKE 1757 – 1827

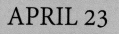

THE LITTLE THINGS?
THE LITTLE
MOMENTS?
THEY AREN'T LITTLE.

JON KABAT-ZINN,
B. 1944

Nothing will
content those
who are not content
with a little.

GREEK PROVERB

APRIL 24

I am done with great things
and big plans, great institutions
and big success.
I am for those tiny, invisible
loving human forces that work
from individual to individual,
creeping through the crannies
of the world
like so many rootlets...

WILLIAM JAMES 1842 – 1910

SEPTEMBER 10

To be conscious
that you are ignorant is a great
step to knowledge.

BENJAMIN DISRAELI 1804 – 1881

APRIL 25

Enthusiasm moves the world.

J. BALFOUR

SEPTEMBER 9

Life can only
be understood
backwards:
but it must be lived
forwards.

SØREN KIERKEGAARD
1813 – 1855

APRIL 26

If it's working, keep doing it.
If it's not working, stop doing it. If you don't know
what to do, don't do anything.

DR. MELVIN KONNER

Do not spoil what you have by desiring what you have not; remember that what you now have was once among the things you only hoped for.

EPICURUS
341 B.C. - 270 B.C.

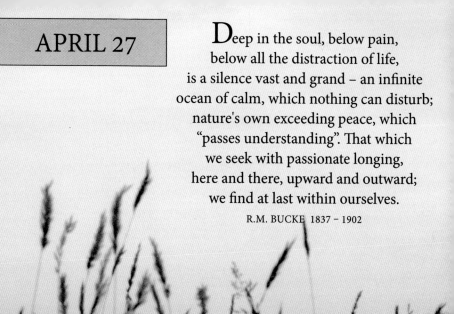

APRIL 27

Deep in the soul, below pain,
below all the distraction of life,
is a silence vast and grand – an infinite
ocean of calm, which nothing can disturb;
nature's own exceeding peace, which
"passes understanding". That which
we seek with passionate longing,
here and there, upward and outward;
we find at last within ourselves.

R.M. BUCKE 1837 – 1902

SEPTEMBER 7

The three great vices seem to be efficiency,
punctuality, and the desire for achievement and success.
They are the things that make people
so unhappy and so nervous.

LIN YUTANG 1895 – 1976

APRIL 28

Love alone is capable of uniting living beings in such a way
as to complete and fulfil them, for it alone
takes them and joins them by what is deepest in themselves.

PIERRE TEILHARD DE CHARDIN 1881 – 1955

SEPTEMBER 6

I like living.
I have sometimes
been wildly,
despairingly,
acutely miserable,
racked with sorrow,
but through it all
I still know quite
certainly that just
to be alive is a
grand thing.

AGATHA CHRISTIE
1890 - 1976

How simple and frugal
a thing is happiness:
a glass of wine, a roast chestnut,
a wretched little brazier,
the sound of the sea...
All that is required to feel
that here and now is happiness
is a simple, frugal heart.

NIKOS KAZANTZAKIS
1883 – 1957

SEPTEMBER 5

Don't hurry,
don't worry.
You're only here
for a short visit.
So be sure
to stop and smell
the flowers.

WALTER HAGEN
1892 – 1969

FORTUNE
COMES
TO THOSE
WHO SMILE.

JAPANESE WISDOM

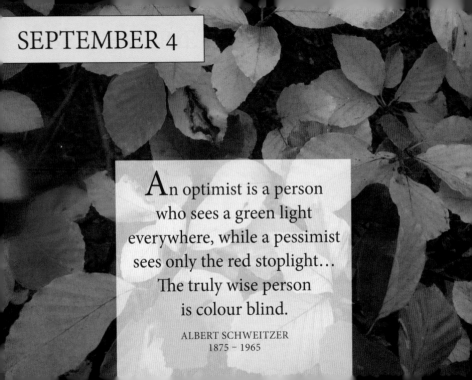

An optimist is a person
who sees a green light
everywhere, while a pessimist
sees only the red stoplight...
The truly wise person
is colour blind.

ALBERT SCHWEITZER
1875 – 1965

MAY 1

Over all the mountaintops
is peace. In all treetops
you perceive scarcely
a breath. The little birds
in the forest are silent.
Wait then; soon you, too,
will have peace.

JOHANN WOLFGANG VON GOETHE
1749 – 1832

I have just three
things to teach:
simplicity, patience,
compassion.
These three
are your
greatest treasure.

LAO TZU
604 B.C. – 531 B.C.

Genius is the ability
to reduce the complicated
to the simple.

C. W. CERAM

"If only you could make now last forever,"
Frank said on one of those nights while they lay on their backs
watching a huge half-moon roar up out of the dark shoulders
of the mountain. Frank was eleven and not by nature a philosopher.
They had all lain still, thinking about this for a while.
Somewhere, a long way off, a coyote called.
"I guess that's all forever is," his father replied.
"Just one long trail of nows. And I guess all you can do is try
and live one now at a time without getting too worked up about
the last now or the next now." It seemed to Tom as good a recipe
for life as he'd yet heard.

NICHOLAS EVANS, B. 1950

MAY 3

To be clever is
not necessarily
to be wise.
Wisdom is rooted
in empathy,
a concern for
all living things.

PAM BROWN 1928 – 2014

SEPTEMBER 1

The world is round and the place which may seem
like the end may also be the beginning.

IVY BAKER PRIEST 1905 ~ 1975

Ecstasy is an idea, a goal, but it can be the expectation of every day. Those times when we're grounded in our body, pure in our heart, clear in our mind, rooted in our soul, and suffused with the energy, the spirit of life, are our birthright. It's really not that hard to stop and luxuriate in the joy and wonder of being.

GABRIELLE ROTH 1941 – 2012

AUGUST 31

You cannot do
a kind thing
too soon, for you
never know
how soon you
will be too late.

RALPH WALDO EMERSON
1803 – 1882

MAY 5

Forgiveness is
the answer
to the child's dream
of a miracle by
which what is broken
is made whole again,
what is soiled is again
made clean.

DAG HAMMARSKJÖLD
1905 – 1961

AUGUST 30

If we have not quiet
in our minds,
outward comfort
will do no more for us
than a golden slipper
on a gouty foot.

JOHN BUNYAN 1628 – 1688

MAY 6

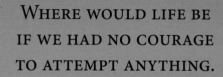

WHERE WOULD LIFE BE
IF WE HAD NO COURAGE
TO ATTEMPT ANYTHING.

VINCENT VAN GOGH
1853 – 1890

AUGUST 29

STORMS
MAKE
OAKS
TAKE
DEEPER
ROOT.

GEORGE HERBERT
1593–1633

The thoughts we choose to think
are the tools we use to paint the canvas
of our lives.

LOUISE L. HAY, B. 1926

AUGUST 28

Nature is painting for us, day after day, pictures of infinite beauty if only we have eyes to see them....

JOHN RUSKIN 1819 ~ 1900

MAY 8

Learn appreciation.
Be willing to take lovingly
each small gift of life
and receive it and
acknowledge that you
have received it,
and appreciate it and allow
it in. You won't be happy
with more until you're
happy with what you've got.

VIKI KING

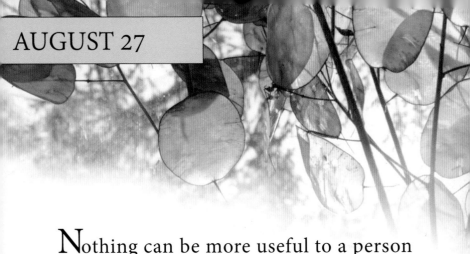

Nothing can be more useful to a person
than a determination not to be hurried.

HENRY DAVID THOREAU 1817 – 1862

MAY 9

Life could not continue,
without throwing
the past into the past,
liberating the present
from its burden.

PAUL TILLICH 1886 – 1965

One person with knowledge of his or her life's purpose is more powerful than ten thousand working without that knowledge.

MUHAMMAD ALI, B. 1942

MAY 10

You are as young as your faith, as old as your doubts,
as young as your self-confidence, as old as your fear,
as young as your hope, as old as your despair.

SAMUEL ULLMAN 1840 – 1924

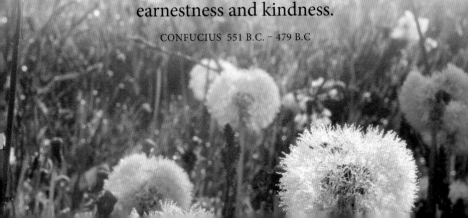

AUGUST 25

To be able to practise five things
everywhere constitutes perfect virtue...
gravity, generosity of soul, sincerity,
earnestness and kindness.

CONFUCIUS 551 B.C. – 479 B.C

The secret of success, of happiness
is to value every moment of each day.

PAM BROWN 1928 – 2014

AUGUST 24

To be without some of the things you want
is an indispensable part of happiness.

BERTRAND RUSSELL 1872 – 1970

MAY 12

I compared notes with one
of my friends who expects
everything of the universe,
and is disappointed when
anything is less than the best,
and I found that I begin
at the other extreme,
expecting nothing, and am
always full of thanks for
moderate goods.

RALPH WALDO EMERSON
1803 – 1882

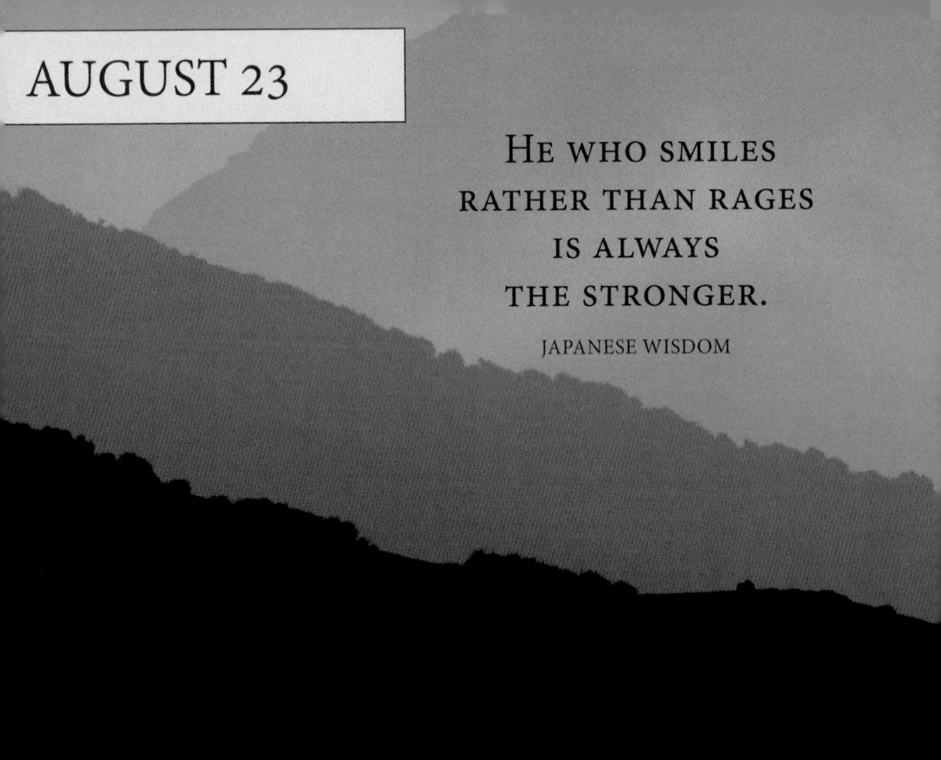

HE WHO SMILES
RATHER THAN RAGES
IS ALWAYS
THE STRONGER.

JAPANESE WISDOM

They who give have all things;
they who withhold have nothing.

HINDU PROVERB

Look for a lovely thing
and you will find it,
It is not far –
It never will be far.

SARA TEASDALE 1884 – 1933

It is difficult to live in the present,
ridiculous to live
in the future and impossible
to live in the past.

JIM BISHOP 1907 – 1987

AUGUST 21

Loss is life's non-negotiable side. It is the time when we learn, unconditionally, that we are powerless over things we thought we had a grip on. But it doesn't stop there, because every ending brings a new beginning.

STEPHANIE ERICSSON

MAY 15

To love is to risk
not being loved in return.
To hope is to risk
disappointment.
But risks must be taken
because the greatest
risk in life is to risk nothing.

AUTHOR UNKNOWN

Life itself is the proper binge.

JULIA CHILD 1912 – 2004

MAY 16

What lies behind us,and what lies before us are tiny matters, compared to what lies within us.

RALPH WALDO EMERSON 1803 – 1882

AUGUST 19

Courage is the price
that Life exacts for
granting peace.
The soul that knows it not,
knows no release from
little things; knows not
the livid loneliness of fear.

AMELIA EARHART 1898 – 1937

MAY 17

"If only I had..." can destroy a life.

PAM BROWN 1928 – 2014

AUGUST 18

Look to give happiness and you will find it.

PAM BROWN 1928 – 2014

MAY 18

The white fathers told us:
"I think, therefore I am"
and the black woman
within each of us – the poet –
whispers in our dreams,
I feel, therefore I can be free.

AUDRE LORDE 1934 – 1992

AUGUST 17

THERE IS NO DUTY
WE SO MUCH
UNDERRATE
AS THE DUTY OF
BEING HAPPY.

ROBERT LOUIS STEVENSON
1850 – 1894

MAY 19

Perfection of character is this: to live each day as if it were your last, without frenzy, without apathy, without pretence.

MARCUS AURELIUS
A.D. 121 – 180

Treasure the love you receive above all.
It will survive long after your gold
and good health have vanished.

OG MANDINO 1923 – 1996

MAY 20

To miss
the joy
is to
miss all.

ROBERT LOUIS STEVENSON
1850-1894

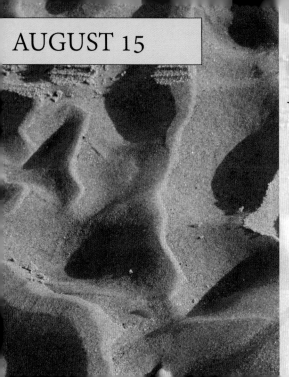

AUGUST 15

You can outdistance
that which is
running after you
but not what is
running inside you.

RWANDAN PROVERB

MAY 21

Hold tightly
to possessions.
Hold tightly
to friendship.
Hold gently
to love.

PAM BROWN 1928 – 2014

AUGUST 14

Never feel self-pity, the most destructive emotion
there is. How awful to be caught up in the
terrible squirrel cage of self.

MILLICENT FENWICK 1910 – 1992

THE ONE WHO MASTERS THE GREY EVERYDAY IS A HERO.

FYODOR MIKHAILOVICH DOSTOYEVSKY
1821 – 1881

AUGUST 13

Nothing great was ever achieved without enthusiasm. The way of life is wonderful; it is by abandonment.

RALPH WALDO EMERSON 1803 – 1882

MAY 23

All the great things
are simple, and many
can be expressed in
a single word:
freedom; justice;
honour; duty;
mercy; hope.

SIR WINSTON CHURCHILL
1874 – 1965

The submissive overcomes the hard.
Everyone in the world knows yet no one can put
this knowledge into practice.

LAO TZU 604 B.C. – 531 B.C.

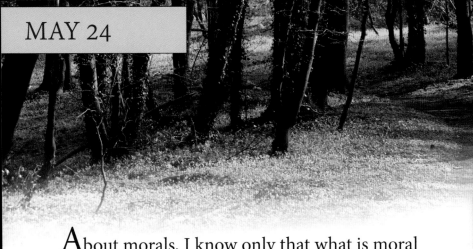

MAY 24

About morals, I know only that what is moral
is what you feel good after and what is immoral
is what you feel bad after.

ERNEST HEMINGWAY 1898 – 1961

AUGUST 11

The heart
has its reasons
which reason
knows
nothing of.

BLAISE PASCAL 1623 – 1662

Is not life a hundred times
too short for us to bore ourselves?

FRIEDRICH WILHELM NIETZSCHE
1844 – 1900

AUGUST 10

It is easier to be ignorant
than to learn to reason.
It is easier to accept
the opinions of others
than to examine
and question their
arguments.
Be brave.
Don't take the easier way.
Think for yourself.

PAM BROWN 1928 – 2014

MAY 26

Demand much
of yourself
and expect little
of others.
Thus you will
be spared
much vexation.

CONFUCIUS
551 B.C. – 479 B.C.

AUGUST 9

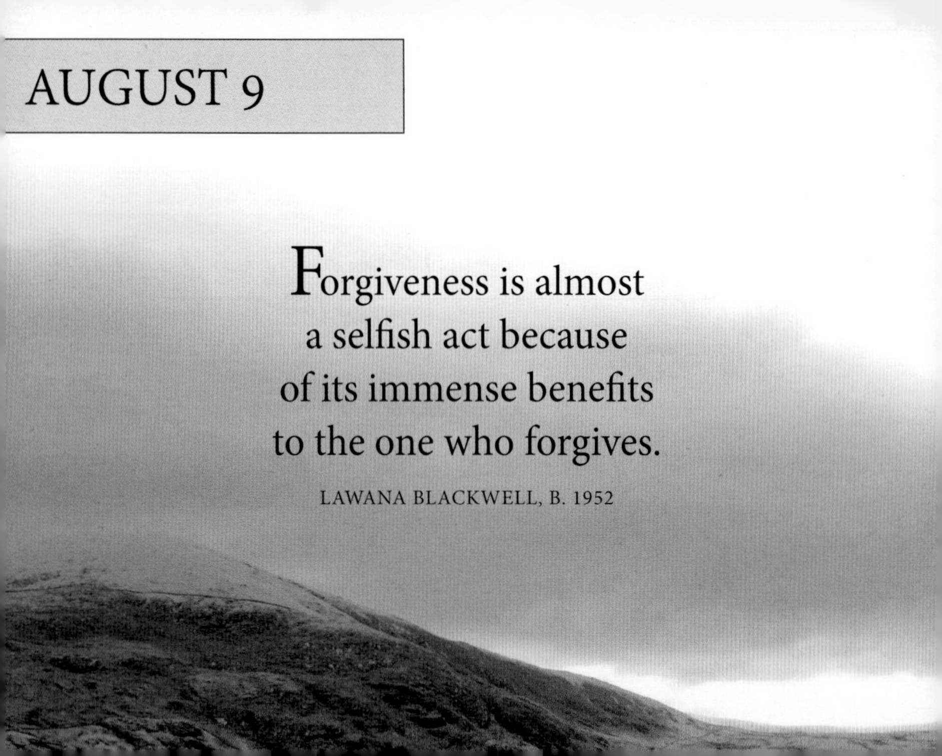

Forgiveness is almost
a selfish act because
of its immense benefits
to the one who forgives.

LAWANA BLACKWELL, B. 1952

MAY 27

All the goals
and targets in the world
mean nothing unless
you're happy,
you love
and you're loved.

DARIUS DANESH, B. 1980

AUGUST 8

How many days does
one have in one's life?
What a pity if you
do not act today.
Don't say you can put
things off till tomorrow.
For tomorrow you'll
have other things to do.

WEN JIA

MAY 28

EACH DAY
THE FIRST DAY:
EACH DAY
A LIFE.

DAG HAMMARSKJÖLD
1905 – 1961

AUGUST 7

When you carry out acts
of kindness you get
a wonderful feeling inside.
It is as though something
inside your body responds
and says, Yes, this is how
I ought to feel.

RABBI
HAROLD S. KUSHNER,
B. 1935

MAY 29

There is so much
in the world for us all
if we only have the eyes
to see it, and the heart
to love it, and
the hand to gather
it to ourselves…

LUCY MAUD MONTGOMERY
1874 – 1942

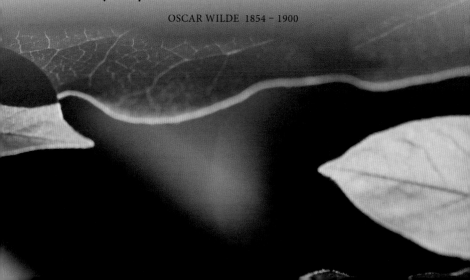

AUGUST 6

The true mystery of the world is the visible not the invisible.

OSCAR WILDE 1854 - 1900

MAY 30

I expect to pass
through life but once.
If therefore, there
be any kindness,
I can show, or any good
thing I can do to any fellow
being, let me do it now,
and not defer or neglect it,
as I shall not pass
this way again.

WILLIAM PENN 1644 – 1718

AUGUST 5

Always remember
two important things…
all we have is each other.
And the only moment
in time which
is ours is now.

FROM
"THE FRIENDSHIP BOOK
OF FRANCIS GAY"

MAY 31

When you're through learning, you're through.

VERNON LAW, B. 1932

AUGUST 4

Many a man
would rather
you heard his story
than granted
his request.

LORD CHESTERFIELD
1694 – 1773

JUNE 1

EVERY ONE OF US
IS A WONDER.
EVERY ONE OF US
HAS A STORY.

KRISTIN HUNTER, B. 1931

Refuse to pander to a morbid interest in your own misdeeds.
Pick yourself up, be sorry, shake yourself, and go on again.

EVELYN UNDERHILL 1875 – 1941

JUNE 2

When one door
shuts
another opens.

SAMUEL PALMER
1805 – 1881

AUGUST 2

Everyone must row
with the oars he has.

PROVERB

JUNE 3

Success makes
life easier.
It doesn't make
living easier...

BRUCE SPRINGSTEEN B. 1949

AUGUST 1

The pursuit of happiness is a most ridiculous phrase:
if you pursue happiness you'll never find it.

C. P. SNOW 1905 – 1980

JUNE 4

Do a thing at its time and peace follows it.

MANDINKA PROVERB

JULY 31

Only the most wise person in the world can unite the quickness, clarity, breadth and depth of understanding needed for guiding others; the magnanimity, generosity, benevolence, and gentleness needed for getting along with others, the serenity, seriousness, unwaveringness and the well-informedness and thoroughness needed for exercising sound judgement.

CONFUCIUS 551 B.C. – 479 B.C.

JUNE 5

If success depends
upon misusing those
about you – opt for failure!

PAM BROWN 1928 – 2014

JULY 30

There is nothing to be gained by wishing you were someplace else or waiting for a better situation. You see where you are and you do what you can with that.

JACOB K. JAVITS 1904 – 1986

JUNE 6

Aerodynamically,
the bumble bee shouldn't
be able to fly,
but the bumble bee
doesn't know it so it
goes on flying anyway.

MARY KAY ASH 1915 – 2001

JULY 29

"Henry Rackmeyer,
you tell us what is important."
"A shaft of sunlight at the end
of a dark afternoon,
a note in music,
and the way the back of
a baby's neck smells...."
"Correct," said Stuart.
"Those are the
important things."

E. B. WHITE 1899 – 1985

JUNE 7

Wʜᴀᴛ ʟɪꜰᴇ ᴄᴀɴ
ᴄᴏᴍᴘᴀʀᴇ ᴛᴏ ᴛʜɪꜱ?
Sɪᴛᴛɪɴɢ ǫᴜɪᴇᴛʟʏ
ʙʏ ᴛʜᴇ ᴡɪɴᴅᴏᴡ,
I ᴡᴀᴛᴄʜ
ᴛʜᴇ ʟᴇᴀᴠᴇꜱ ꜰᴀʟʟ
ᴀɴᴅ ᴛʜᴇ ꜰʟᴏᴡᴇʀꜱ
ʙʟᴏᴏᴍ,
Aꜱ ᴛʜᴇ ꜱᴇᴀꜱᴏɴꜱ
ᴄᴏᴍᴇ ᴀɴᴅ ɢᴏ.

Hꜱᴜᴇʜ Tᴏᴜ 982 – 1052

Execute every act of thy life as though it were thy last.

MARCUS AURELIUS 121 – 180

It takes no more time to see the good side
of life than it takes to see the bad.

JIMMY BUFFETT

JULY 27

Every area of trouble
gives out a ray of hope,
and the one
unchangeable certainty
is that nothing
is certain
or unchangeable.

PRESIDENT JOHN F. KENNEDY
1917 – 1963

JUNE 9

Do not come to the end of your life only to find
you have not lived. For many come to the point of leaving
the space of the earth and when they gaze back,
they see the joy and the beauty
that could not be theirs because of the fears they lived.

CLEARWATER

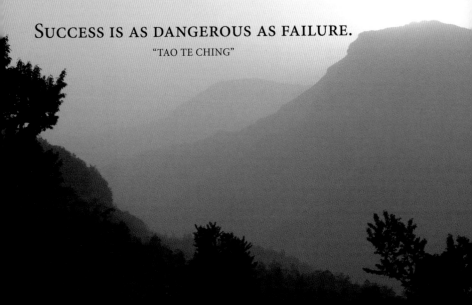

JULY 26

SUCCESS IS AS DANGEROUS AS FAILURE.
"TAO TE CHING"

Hope's highly unlikely to serve you happiness on a plate, just because you wish or want it so. Yes, it's wonderful to hope for love, success and adventure. But to make them real, go and search for them, work at them, make them yours. Make your hopes and dreams real.

DR. DALTON EXLEY

The act of longing for something will always be more intense than the requiting of it.

GAIL GODWIN, B. 1937

We can easily manage, if we only take each day, the burden appointed for it. But the load will be too heavy for us if we carry yesterday's burden over again today...

JOHN NEWTON 1725 – 1807

JULY 24

Each second
you can be reborn.
Each second there
can be a new
beginning.
It is choice.
It is your choice.

CLEARWATER

JUNE 12

Measure your health by your
sympathy with morning and Spring.
If there is no response in you to the
awakening of nature, if the prospect
of an early morning walk does not
banish sleep, if the warble of the first
bluebird does not thrill you,
you know that the morning
and spring of your life are past.
Thus may you feel your pulse.

HENRY DAVID THOREAU 1817 – 1862

JULY 23

Keep company with those who
may make you a better person.

ENGLISH PROVERB

JUNE 13

KEEP A GREEN
TREE IN YOUR
HEART AND
PERHAPS THE
SINGING BIRD
WILL COME.

CHINESE
PROVERB

I AM STILL
LEARNING.

MICHELANGELO
1475 – 1564

Life is short and we have not
too much time for
gladdening the hearts
of those who are travelling
the dark way with us.
Oh, be swift to love!
Make haste to be kind.

HENRI FRÉDÉRIC AMIEL
1821 – 1881

Appreciation is
a wonderful thing.
It makes what is
excellent in others
belong to us as well.

VOLTAIRE 1694 – 1778

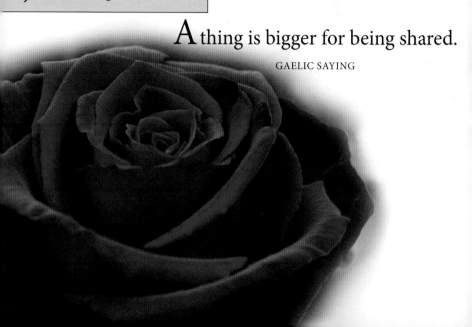

A thing is bigger for being shared.

GAELIC SAYING

Growth itself contains the germ of happiness.

PEARL S. BUCK 1892 – 1973

Y ou grow up the day
you have your first real
laugh at yourself.

ETHEL BARRYMORE
1879 – 1959

JULY 19

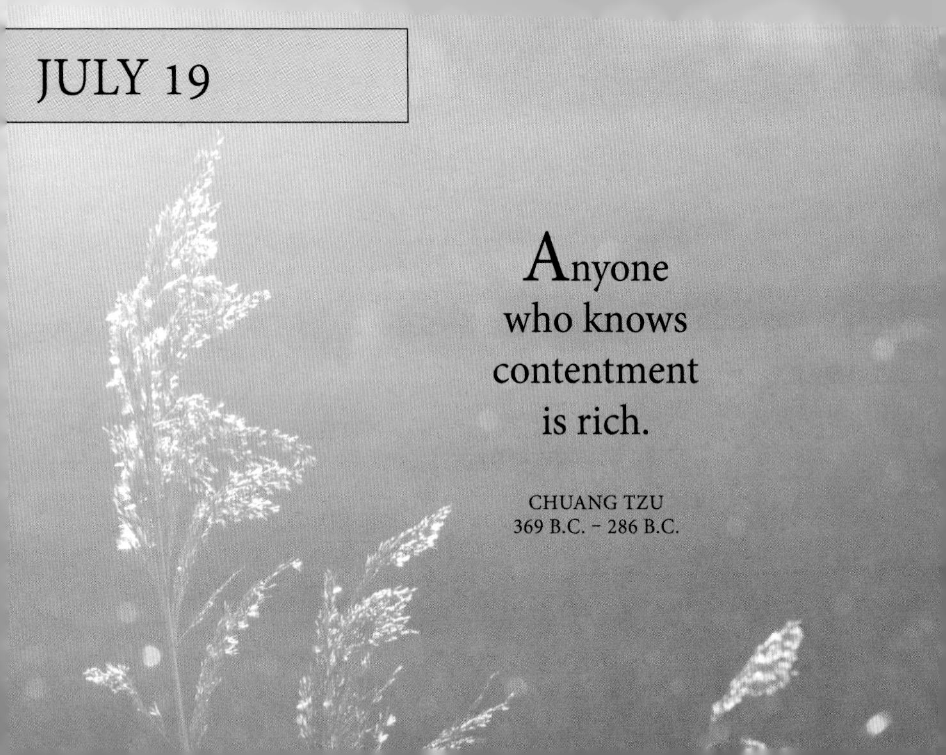

Anyone
who knows
contentment
is rich.

CHUANG TZU
369 B.C. – 286 B.C.

Some people are always grumbling because roses have thorns; I am thankful that thorns have roses.

ALPHONSE KARR
1808 – 1890

JULY 18

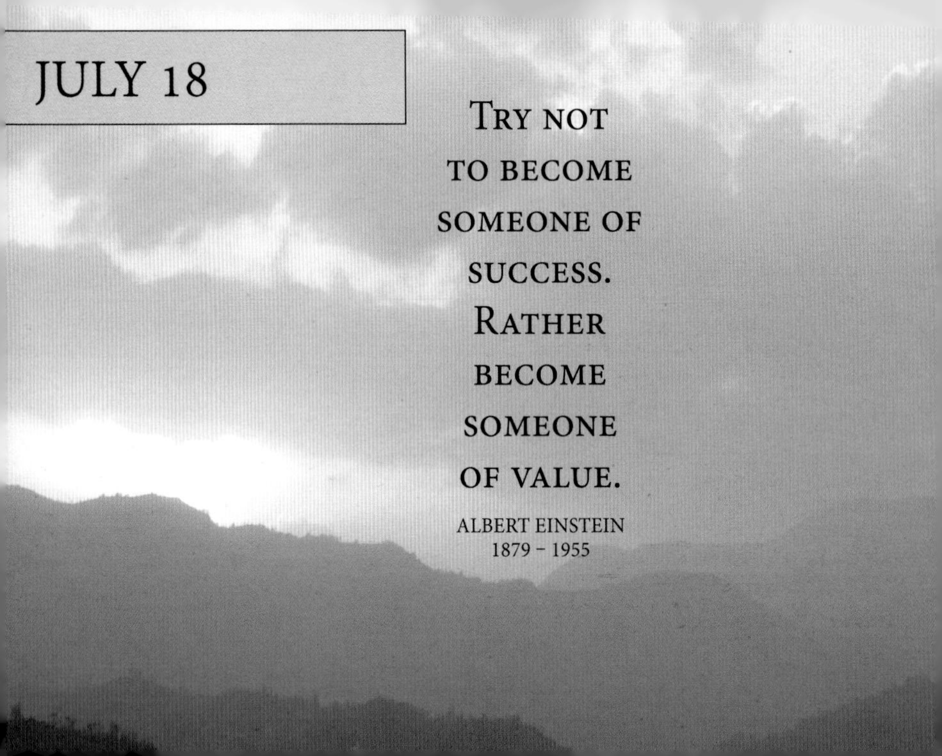

TRY NOT
TO BECOME
SOMEONE OF
SUCCESS.
RATHER
BECOME
SOMEONE
OF VALUE.

ALBERT EINSTEIN
1879 – 1955

JUNE 18

You ask why I make my home
in the mountain forest,
and I smile, and am silent,
and even my soul remains
quiet: it lives in the other
world which no one owns.
The peach trees blossom.
The water flows.

LI PO 701 – 762

JULY 17

Learn the sweet
magic of
a cheerful face;
Not always smiling,
but at least serene.

OLIVER
WENDELL HOLMES SNR.
1809 – 1894

JUNE 19

The most
important thing
in communication
is to hear what
isn't being said.

PETER F. DRUCKER
1909 − 2003

JULY 16

One of the deepest
secrets of life
is that all that
is really worth doing
is what we do
for others.

LEWIS CARROLL 1832 – 1898

Happiness is not acquired; it does not consist in appearances. We each have to build it during every moment of our lives, working through our hearts.

WOMAN ELDER
IN A DOGON VILLAGE

All the adversity
I've had in my life,
all my troubles
and obstacles,
have strengthened me...
You may not realize it
when it happens,
but a kick in the teeth
may be the best thing
in the world for you.

WALT DISNEY 1901 – 1966

IT'S A VERY SHORT TRIP.
WHILE ALIVE, LIVE!

MALCOLM S. FORBES
1919 – 1990

Better to say
but a few words,
but filled with meaning,
than to speak many
that are but idle sounds
and as easy to utter
as they are useless.

VINCENT VAN GOGH
1853 – 1890

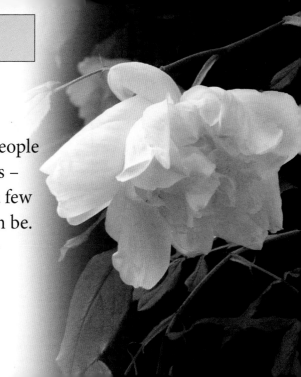

JUNE 22

We have enough people
who tell it like it is –
now we could use a few
who tell it like it can be.

ROBERT ORBEN, B. 1927

JULY 13

Make three lists:
the things you have to do,
want to do, and neither
have to do nor want to do.
Then, for the rest
of your life,
forget everything
in the third category.

ROBERT S. ELIOT
& DENNIS L. BREO

JUNE 23

There are moments
when everything goes well;
don't be frightened,
it won't last.

JULES RENARD
1894 – 1910

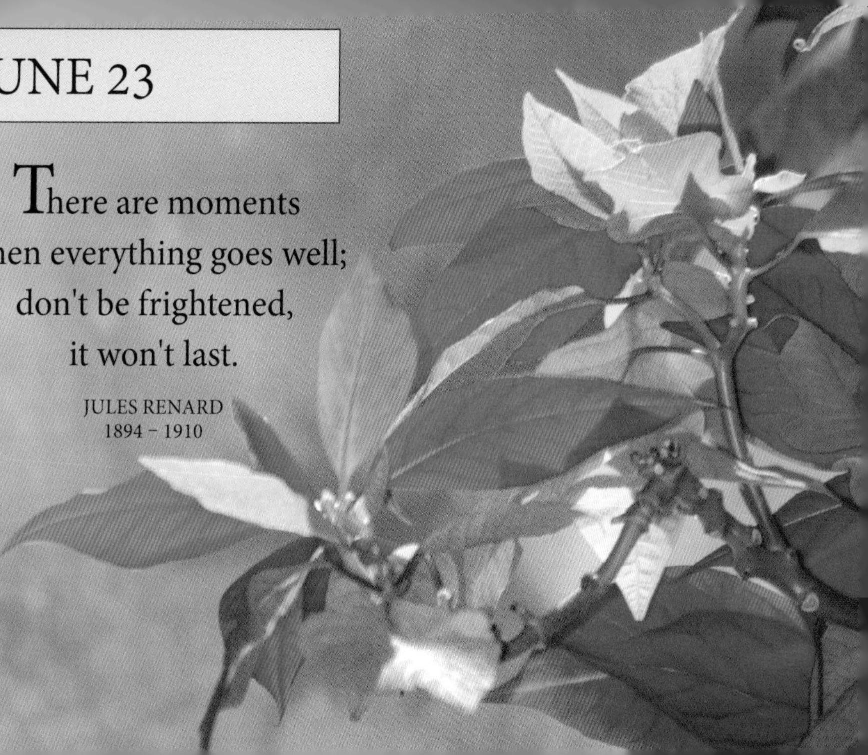

JULY 12

Live today
as if there were
no tomorrow.
Live tomorrow
as if there were
no today.

STUART & LINDA MACFARLANE

JUNE 24

Getting what you
go after is success;
but liking it while
you are getting it
is happiness.

BERTHA DAMON

JULY 11

There is no
good reason
why we should not
develop and change
until the last day
we live.

KAREN HORNEY
1885 – 1952

Let us go singing as far as we go: the road will be less tedious.

VIRGIL 70 B.C. - 19 B.C.

JULY 10

PEOPLE
THAT VALUE
PRIVILEGES
ABOVE
PRINCIPLES
SOON LOSE
BOTH.

DWIGHT D. EISENHOWER
1890 – 1969

On the most
exalted throne
in the world,
we are still seated
on nothing
but our arse!

MICHEL DE MONTAIGNE
1533 – 1592

May success never
blur your vision.
May failure only
teach you how
to begin again.

PAM BROWN 1928 – 2014

Ordinary people, ordinary kindness,
keep the dark at bay.

PAM BROWN 1928 – 2014

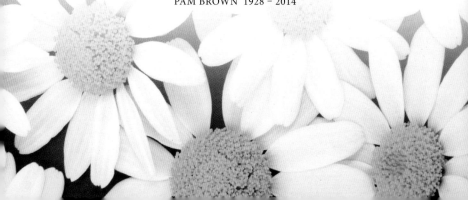

JULY 8

Nothing good is ever lost. It is a thread of gold that brightens the tapestry that is life.

PAM BROWN 1928 – 2014

JUNE 28

Toleration...
is the greatest gift of
the mind; it requires
the same effort of
the brain that it takes
to balance
oneself on a bicycle.

HELEN KELLER
1880 – 1968

Heroism is the brilliant
triumph of the soul
over the flesh –
that is to say, over fear...
Heroism is the dazzling
and brilliant concentration
of courage.

HENRI FRÉDÉRIC AMIEL
1821 – 1881

JUNE 29

If you want happiness
for an hour – take a nap.
If you want happiness
for a day – go walking.
If you want happiness
for a lifetime -
help someone else.

CHINESE PROVERB

JULY 6

Set your goals
high and aim
for the stars,
but be humble
enough to accept –
graciously –
that it's fine
and desirable
to fall short.

ANNA FREUD
1895 - 1982

If one does not know
to which port one is sailing,
no wind is favourable.

SENECA THE YOUNGER
4 B.C. – A.D. 65

JULY 5

If you are wise, laugh.

MARTIAL c.40 – c.104

THE PATH UP AND DOWN
IS ONE AND THE SAME.

HERACLITUS
535 B.C. – 475 B.C.

JULY 4

It is common for the originator of a benefit to forget his good act, and that is fine. What is damnable and unspeakable is for the beneficiary of that good act to forget it.

AMADOU HAMPÂTÉ BÂ
1901 – 1991

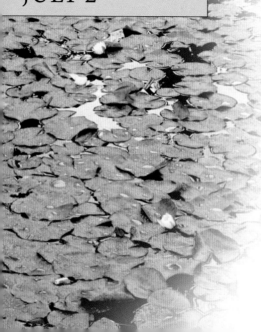

JULY 2

GREED
AND WISDOM
CANNOT
SHARE
A BED.

PAM BROWN
1928 – 2014

Humans have never been
so unhappy as at this moment
when we are
accumulating so much.

CHEIKH HAMIDOU KANE